THE TWO MCNAUGHTENS

Borgo Press Books by JEAN-FRANÇOIS REGNARD

The Two McNaughtens

THE TWO MCNAUGHTENS

A PLAY IN THREE ACTS

JEAN-FRANÇOIS REGNARD

Translated and Adapted by Frank J. Morlock

THE BORGO PRESS
MMXIII

THE TWO MCNAUGHTENS

Copyright © 1986, 2013 by Frank J. Morlock

FIRST BORGO PRESS EDITION

Published by Wildside Press LLC

www.wildsidebooks.com

DEDICATION

For Sami Caldwell—
my very good friend in San Miguel

CONTENTS

CAST OF CHARACTERS. 9
ACT I, Scene 1 11
ACT I, Scene 2 37
ACT II, Scene 3. 65
ACT II, Scene 4. 95
ACT III, Scene 5 123
ABOUT THE TRANSLATOR. 147

CAST OF CHARACTERS

McNaughten

Captain McNaughten

Mr. Hastings, Flavella's father

Flavella Hastings

Urania, Mr. Hastings' older sister

Jenny, Urania's maid

Spruce, the Captain's valet

Mr. Torrington, a solicitor

Squire

Mr. Bronlow, a merchant

ACT I
SCENE 1

A street in London. Captain McNaughten comes in, looking for his valet.

Captain

I am quite beside myself. A curse on Spruce! I think he was born for the sole purpose of enraging me. I am not going to put up with him any longer. The scoundrel always tries my patience to the limits. He knows very well that I am waiting for him on tenterhooks— But now I see him coming. Where have you been, rogue? Tell me.

(Spruce enters, carrying a heavy trunk which he first puts down and then sits on, without responding to the Captain.)

Captain

Speak, reply!

Spruce

For the moment, sir, I have nothing to say. Let me get my breath a moment, please—I'm totally winded.

Captain

Do you always intend to put me in a fury and then play with me? I don't know what prevents me from giving you a beating. What, you rogue, just to go off to the custom house to get my trunk, takes you all day?

Spruce

Oh, sir, customs inspectors are terrible men. All the savages in the world are less barbarous. They can only talk in monosyllables. "yes, no, what, sir? I have no time. But, sir— Would you kindly open up—" They need maybe a hundred words in their vocabulary. They give me a headache. Finally, when you need them for something, they're more proud and stuck up than an archbishop.

Captain

What! Do you mean to pretend you stayed at the customs house until just now?

Spruce

Oh, no. Seeing the customs inspector was about to take more than an hour—besides, he had a disagreeable phiz—I preferred to wait at a tavern.

Captain

Your yen for brew always gets the best of you. Does wine command you always?

Spruce

Everyone has his weakness, sir— As you are well aware. It's the bad example more than the brew that puts me down the wrong road. I'd really like to live a clean life—

Captain

Why do you always keep bad company, then?

Spruce

I've made several efforts to avoid it—all in vain. I like you a lot and I don't want to leave you.

Captain

What's that, scoundrel?

Spruce

Sir, an ancient custom of speaking my mind gives me the right. My case is like your own. I've seen you drunk more than once in a tavern, and many's the time I had to help you home to bed. I've never scolded you much about these little escapades—we ought not to mention other people's infirmities— Forget them, since they forget ours.

Captain

I'll forgive you for liking your bottle—if I thought that was your only vice—but your penchant for one sin carries you on to a thousand others. You have a strange passion for gambling.

Spruce

Oh, if I gamble a little it's only to spend the time while you are spending the night in certain black gambling dens.

I hear you swearing right up to the door. I swear, too, when luck is against me. And who can tell us apart? You swear in your room, and I swear on the stairs. I imitate you in every respect. You drink, gamble, and love with extreme passion, and I drink, gamble—and love a little, too. And if I am a flirt, it's because you are one, too.

Consummate in the art, I might add. You go every day with a vagabond ardor, raffling off all the ladies—from blonde to brunette. Today, Flavella dominates you— you say you love her—but I don't know why.

Captain

You don't know why! Is it possible you refuse to render homage to her charms, to her divine eyes? I saw her at her aunt's, where I was quite enchanted. She wounded me to the heart.

Spruce

Yet you have an attentive soul for her crazy Aunt—Urania. Now I approve of Urania. Perfect choice. Without her money we'd be in an awful fix. Meanwhile, I profit, too. You cajole the Aunt, and I corrupt Jenny, her maid—

Thus, you see—

Captain

Yes, I see—in a word, you think you know everything. You are nothing but a nearsighted fool! To prevent yourself from uttering some new stupidity, shut up, and take my trunk to the hotel.

Spruce (picking up the trunk)

I obey. But if I should want to speak on this vain subject again, believe me, I can hold forth at some length.

Captain

Oh, be quiet!

Spruce

When I have a mind to, I can speak better than anybody—

Captain

Wait! Whose trunk is this?

Spruce

Huh! By George, it's yours.

Captain

It doesn't in the least look like mine.

Spruce

For a while, I had the same suspicion as you. But it's got your name and address on it—and that relieved my mind of any doubt. (puts the trunk down) Here, read the words very plainly written. "To McNaughten, London."

Captain

True, but wait a bit—what do you say to this? It's not my handwriting. Therefore, it is not my trunk.

Spruce

You're right. But it resembles your handwriting a great deal.

Captain

You acted impulsively in taking this trunk.

Spruce

But, sir, do you take me for a fool? In returning from Flanders, where you had an abrupt discharge from your regiment, did I not put the trunk, at your instruction, on a stage coach bound for London, so that we might travel more quickly. And didn't I obey you? I've done everything right in this whole business. No reproaches, please.

Captain

We'll soon see whether this was your fault or not. Open it up and let's try to get to the bottom of this mystery.

Spruce (taking out a ring of keys)

Sir, in a second, I am going to satisfy you. (trying a key) My goodness! The key doesn't fit.

Captain

Break it open.

Spruce

If you want me to, I won't object. Let's begin proceedings. (after some efforts, Spruce manages to open the trunk)

(Spruce looks in and stares)

Captain

What's wrong with you? Look at me.

Spruce (bewildered)

I don't see any of your clothes in here!

Captain

What the—wretch?

Spruce

Sir, there's no need to be testy. The swap we've made may be better for us. I don't believe you had clothes like these in your trunk.

(displaying some expensive clothing)

Captain

And my letters, scoundrel, my letters from Flavella? The letters in which she expressed her love for me?

Who will give them back to me—tell me!

Spruce (removing a packet of letters from the trunk)

Wait—perhaps you will find consolation in these.

Captain

Do you know that jokesters and comedians usually waste their time with me?

(The Captain reads the letters while Spruce inventories the clothes.)

Spruce

My intent was not to put you in a temper—but without losing time we must make our inventory. This costume for chicanery surely belonged to some Scotsman, and this is an Irish peasant. (displaying clothes) Now, this one is rather modish—usable for a hunt, I think.

Captain

Oh, Heavens!

Spruce (startled by the Captain's outburst)

Where will all this thing end?

Captain

This adventure isn't easily believed.

Spruce

Sir, what's wrong with you—are you getting dizzy?

Captain

It's a miracle. You won't believe it when I tell you.

Spruce

Sir, I will, I promise you—if you don't lie.

Captain

As you know, I was born a McNaughten, near Edinburgh. I am of a blood which ceded valor to no one. You know that having lost father, mother, and relatives, and penniless, I was left to spend my days in the Highlands. To escape, I joined the army when I was only fifteen. Only I had a brother, who lived with me in the home of my uncle—a rich old miser who wouldn't give me a penny. So I ran away, and they haven't heard of me for many years. And I've heard from many sources that both my brother and my uncle thought me dead.

Spruce

I know all that. And I know your mother died in giving birth to you and that same brother. You and your brother are as indistinguishable as two glasses of milk. In short, you are twins. So what?

Captain

We look so much alike that the finest painters would be easily deceived. Even our own father considered putting a sign on us to tell us apart.

Spruce

I've heard the story of your life several times. What has that story got to do with our present troubles?

Captain

You will be astonished. This trunk belongs to my brother!

Spruce

How about that?

Captain

And I learn from this letter that our uncle is dead—

Spruce

Amazing—

Captain

—and has left all his money to this twin of mine.

Spruce

That is surprising news—no doubt about it. What good does that do?

Captain

Listen attentively. This is worth a good deal of reflection.

Spruce

I'm listening.

Captain (reading the letter)

"I await you, sir, to pay you the sixty thousand pounds which your uncle has left you by his will, and to marry you to Miss Flavella Hastings, of whom I have spoken to you several times in my letters. The lady likes you very much, and her father is very determined on this marriage. Don't waste time in getting to London. Your very humble servant, Charles Torrington."

Spruce

Now, I begin to see—

Captain

Torrington is the name of the honest solicitor who worked for my father. The date, the envelope, and the name, all confirm my conclusion. My brother is coming to London in response to this letter, and, just like me, put his trunk on the coach. And, of course, the name and address caused your error. I conclude, therefore, not very cleverly, that my brother is, perhaps, already in London.

Spruce

That's probably right. I am stupefied by the surprising effects of chance. Necessity caused me to make a mistake, and our fortune will spring from my stupidity. In a single day, we find a decrepit old uncle buried— who leaves behind him a fortune, which in life, he prevented you from attaining. We also find a brother who will receive the fortune, and relieve you of your lady love. Coincidences like these are capable of overwhelming the cleverest person!

Captain

We've got to put our heads together about this. I have a good feeling about it.

Spruce

We could really use that sixty thousand pounds.

Captain

To have them, we will have to use all our skill. They belong to me as much as to my brother. We must prevent my brother from meeting old Torrington. Go—run—find out—don't lose a minute.

Spruce

You know my zeal and eagerness. If he's in London, I have faithful friends who will know of it in less than an hour.

Captain

I am going to Urania. Unfortunately, she knows I am back. I must still pretend to burn with love for her. She has no idea I'm aflame for Flavella. You know what Urania is like—the old girl loves to break men's hearts. The airs that old woman puts on are really insufferable. In fact, she's crazy and loves to be flattered.

Spruce

You're just the man for that, if I may say so, sir.

Captain

What a ray of hope breaks through for my love. While I'm still uncertain what to do about my brother, I'd best manage her. Go back to the customs house, to the stage coach.

Spruce

If I'm not mistaken, here comes Urania and Jenny now.

Captain

Go, quickly, where I send you.

(Exit Spruce)

(Enter Urania and Jenny, her maid)

Urania

What a joy. We will see Captain McNaughten again today. I cannot stay put. Such excitement—agitates me. How do you think I look, Jenny?

Jenny

Charming. Your beauty surprises, ravishes, carries one away, enchants—. It seems Cupid himself has adjusted your face today.

Urania

This girl always has the best taste. (seeing the Captain) Ah, sir, you here! What a lucky chance—this is better than I had hoped for—what hurries your return? What God brings you back to me?

Captain

Cupid.

Urania

Cupid? The poor child!

Captain

Your lovable presence now fully compensates me for the pain of your prior absence. You, who without art, without aid, appear younger every day.

Urania

Foh! Banterer! Love sometimes recalls a person who is absent to mind. Your charming portrait, which makes all my happiness, consoled me a little during your frightful absence. Did mine have the same effect on you?

Captain

Your face preoccupied me like a ghost, and followed

me everywhere. Night could not hide you from my eyes. And even this night, I recall my dream. In my first sleep, I dreamt I was in a garden at sunrise. There, Aurora shone with her rosy fingers. There on the border of a superb canal, where a hundred frothy waves fell in cascades—seemingly pushed by water nymphs. There, I tell you—reposing on a bed of roses—

Urania (agitated)

What did you see?

Captain

I saw you, on a chair, floating over the waves. You resembled Venus. A hundred Cupids pushed a shell, the winds jested about you—

Jenny

Oh, Heaven. What a lovely dream. (aside) He does this better than I do.

Urania

Finish, finish, I beg you.

Captain

My soul was seized by astonishment.

Jenny (low)

That's not surprising.

Urania (dreamily)

And I was Venus, floating on this canal?

Captain

Yes, Madame, your very self. My mind was taken with the noble spectacle. I went right up to you with no opposition—

Urania

Did I have a noble air, a divine bearing? Speak sincerely.

Captain

The most noble in the world. You seemed a goddess in the flesh.

Urania

And what was I wearing? The goddess's clothes?

Captain

Madame, the goddess does not—

Urania

Ah, ah—

Captain

Unluckily, the goddess suddenly vanished from my sight.

Urania

And were we separated?

Captain

Then, I found myself in a grotto—which art had embellished more than nature. There, in full repose, crowned by flowers, I perceived you reclining on a couch of flowers. I persuaded you of my ardent feelings.

Urania

And—

Captain

You were touched—

Urania

Ah, I was touched—

Captain

By a new goddess. And taking from Venus her natural softness, languorously, you—

Urania

What did I do?

Captain

I don't know. By an unspeakable misfortune, my valet woke me up.

(aside) Whew! I couldn't go any further.

Jenny (aside)

I should take lessons from him, decidedly.

Urania

I am in despair because of this. Servants are always about when we don't want them. Horrid valet.

Captain

Actually, Spruce comes in handy sometimes. But my dream was incomplete. How I wanted to finish it.

Urania

Oh, and I want to finish it, too. To satisfy YOU, so that YOUR happiness will not be a chimera, to quench YOUR flames—after our marriage, of course. But I'm afraid that in the times in which we live, there's a distaste for marriage. Among the men, I mean. But possession alone takes the salt and taste from love.

Captain

Ah, Madame, my love for you is so extreme, I am sure it must last until death. And if, by a misfortune which I cannot prevent, your death should— Ah, great gods, what a frightful despair I would be in. The very thought of it possesses my soul with remorse.

Urania

Let's put that lugubrious idea far away from us. To better celebrate the pleasures of our reunion, I want to dine with you tonight. This morning, I invited a friend—you'll enjoy good company.

Captain

Madame, this honor is very advantageous to me. A small business matter tears me away at present, but I will soon return. I'll hurry.

Urania

Go, my darling. I will await you with impatience.

Captain (bowing, kissing her hand)

Here—in a moment I will return.

(Exit the Captain)

Urania

The love he has for me is not to be imagined.

Jenny (archly)

No, m'am.

Urania

In revenge, I will love him like crazy. How do you like him?

Jenny

He's good-looking. His valet, Spruce, isn't bad to look at, either. We are a little bit in love—but, who's coming—?

It's Mr. Hastings.

(Enter Hastings)

Hastings

Hello, sis.

Urania

Good day, brother, dear.

Hastings

This is lucky, I was going to your house to speak to you on some business.

Urania

This place is as good as any. You won't annoy me.

Hastings

I want to marry Flavella off.

Urania

That's not a bad idea. Your daughter is getting big, you know. People ask me how I can have such a grown-up niece.

Hastings

And our solicitor, Mr. Torrington, whose zeal for our family, you know, has found a good match for her. A young man endowed with wit and character—who possesses more than sixty thousand pounds which he has just inherited from an uncle. Torrington is the trustee of the estate, and has written me that the young heir will arrive today.

Urania

I am truly easy. I think it's a fine idea.

Hastings

This marriage would be a great advantage for our family. So, seeing that you are no longer interested in remarrying, I thought we might endow Flavella with your estate—reserving a life estate for you until your death.

Urania

Until my death! Truly, brother, this project is very appealing to me! I will do no such thing. My death, indeed!

Hastings

But I already sort of promised—

Urania

You promised, eh? Well, DE-promise. I'll have you know, I still think I'm not past marrying and having children—

Hastings

Having children, sis? You're joking, you're past fifty!

Urania

Me! Fifty years old! Me! Jenny!

Jenny (defensively)

Don't blame me. I've never told him your age! Because Madame has lived a while, people think she's no longer young. He's a stupid man.

Hastings

Dear sister, I believe I've been quite fair in my calculations. I reasoned that since you are my elder sister, and I am past fifty myself—necessarily— Therefore, how can I be wrong?

Urania

You're necessarily is stupid. I know very well that it— that it cannot be! My youth is well known. And I can prove it to you, clearly and precisely. My wealth will never be inherited by you. I'll bury you, and your children, and the children I am going to have, too. Despite you and the murderous plots you are hatching. Do you hear, brother dear?— I have spoken. Good day! Come Jenny.

(Exit Urania in a fury)

Hastings

Lovely disposition.

Jenny

Sir, another time—or better yet, say nothing. Or read, if you please, better almanacs. My lady is, still, despite you and your calculations, young and pretty, and all the connoisseurs will remind you of it.

(Exit Jenny)

Hastings

I can see what my sister is up to. Marry again, at her age? The old fool. Well, I have taken some measures. Better go see Torrington and straighten things out. If the man in question is as described, we shall very soon consummate this marriage

BLACKOUT

ACT I
SCENE 2

The same, a short time later. The Captain and Spruce enter from different directions. Spruce is out of breath again.

Spruce

I found your brother, but not without trouble. You see how out of breath I am. I've been around London, from one end to the other—to the stage, to the post, everywhere. And I swear, every street I went down, I met a creditor. I even met that Welshman—the Squire to whom we owe a hundred pounds.

Captain

I am ashamed to owe him for so long. He took me for a gentleman—

Spruce (aside)

Which few do.

Captain

And the first money that I get, I am going to repay him. Nothing will prevent me.

Spruce (aside)

But a wench or a game of cards.

(Aloud)

Wonderful! Anyway, not knowing where to go first, I went back to the custom house. And there I saw your brother—actually knew him instantly from a distance—because of the resemblance. Really, an incredible resemblance. He was arguing with the inspector about the tariff. His face, his features, his bearing, even his tone of voice! If I hadn't known, I would have been deceived completely. But his temper—that's where he's different from you. He's brusque, impolite even— quite unlike you. It's easy to see he isn't a man of the world— in fact, he's a savage brute!

Captain

One shouldn't be surprised by rudeness in a country bumpkin who was nourished without politeness. It will take more than the air of London to get this beastly behavior out of him.

Spruce

As I was saying, I watched his quarrel from a distance, and when he finally left, I gave him a taste of my abilities as a porter. My zeal and flattery worked to such effect that he asked me to be his valet. I even recommended him this lodging—a place fit for the masterful projects I am hatching in my head. He ought to be here any minute.

Captain (amused)

What masterful project are you hatching in that charming head of yours?

Spruce

Fortune herself appeared to me—in total surrender. We can profit by this resemblance you bear to each other to obtain Flavella, and—what's more important—your inheritance. Two birds with one stone.

Captain

Yes, yes, we can. We shall, we will. But how?

Spruce

Nothing could be easier. We'll trade off this bumpkin to Aunt Urania, you will get Miss Flavella, and more important, I will get Jenny.

Captain

And how are we to put this brave plan into action?

Spruce

First, you've got to change clothes, and dress like the heir apparent. Adopt his mannerisms, and the Devil will provide—

Captain

Dress like an heir? My God, I don't know how. I've never been an heir before.

Spruce

Act sad on first sight. Impose on the lawyer and get the money.

Captain

I am a little uncomfortable about deceiving my brother.

Spruce

What an idle and ridiculous delicacy! Risk nothing, gain nothing. Maybe you ought to protect him. With this money, he could do some good—only you don't give him a good character.

Captain

If I want this inheritance, it's only for the sake of Flavella, whom I adore.

Spruce

Of course. And if you don't get it, he will have her! Can you bear thinking of him kissing her?

Captain

Damnation!

Spruce

But he was a fine brother, and you ought not to deceive him.

Captain

He's a son-of-a-bitch. He was always stealing my toys. That's it. I'll do it.

Spruce

Good. That's the spirit.

Captain

I'll tell you what. Flavella doesn't look on me with indifference. Her father knows nothing of it, and, by good luck, has never seen me, because I've never taken the first step to ask for her hand. If I had, all my hopes would have been dashed, I am sure of it. Still, one thing holds me back.

Spruce

Good Heavens, what can it be?

Captain

I've promised in writing to marry Urania.

Spruce

Banish all thought of that engagement. If you were to marry all the women you've promised to marry, you would be a bigamist many times over. Now to work! You must dress like your brother. He's wearing mourning, a little frayed. His wig's a little different than yours, but you really don't need to change much. You must get into mourning, without wasting any time.

Captain

But, Urania is waiting for me to dine with her!

Spruce

You now have other work to do. Dine tomorrow! I believe I see your brother coming up that side street. I'm not mistaken. You must go quick— Double-time,

Captain.

Captain

But, tell me first—

Spruce

I've nothing to say to you now, except go, quickly.

(Reluctantly, with a questioning expression, the Captain goes, hurried off by Spruce. After a moment, enter McNaughten dressed in mourning.)

Spruce

Finally, you're here, sir. To keep my word I've been waiting for you by this hotel, but it's been a long time.

McNaughten

Yes, indeed, here I am. I thought it was all my life was worth to get here. What a country—what a Hell! I made a thousand false turns. I've never run so many risks in my life. One cannot take a step without falling in some trap.

Everywhere some pickpocket hemmed me in. A carriage covered me with mud. What noise, what confusion. I believe that in this city, the Devil has finally settled on his abode.

Spruce

Oh, London is a tumultuous, noisy place.

McNaughten

Really! I'd much prefer to be at a Black Sabbath. A woods full of robbers is a hundred times more secure. My trunk was taken by someone else. I've lost fifteen pounds—and some love letters, too.

Spruce

You have to be on your guard around here.

McNaughten

I believe it, indeed. This loss will make me more alert and exact. Happily, I kept most of my money in my belt.

Spruce

Did you so? How clever of you. (picking his pocket) I've had a bed prepared for you in a nice quiet room, in the back, away from the street. Do you plan to stay in this town long?

McNaughten

The less, the better. I can see nothing to like about it. I'm only here to get married.

Spruce

You usually can't do that business in a single day.

McNaughten

I'm also here to collect an inheritance of sixty thousand pounds. I inherited it from an uncle that I had once, but no longer do—by a singular grace of God.

Spruce

And is it all for you, sir?

McNaughten

Precisely. War took off my brother—opportunely. He was only twenty—in the flower of his youth. He took a quick trip to the promised land, and has never returned. God's grace knows no bounds.

Spruce

Heaven give him peace, and give you success in all your plans. If you have need of my little services, you can employ me, sir, in any way you please. I know London very well, and I am always willing to serve my friends devotedly.

McNaughten

Can you tell me how to find a man named George

Hastings?

Spruce

Hastings?

McNaughten

Exactly, that's his name.

Spruce

Is there a man in London who knows better than I how to get to his house? We'll go together. Have you some business with him?

McNaughten

Yes, I do. By chance, might you also know where a solicitor named Torrington lives?

Spruce

Ah, indeed, I know him. You couldn't have done better than ask me—he's a particular friend of mine. We'll go to him, too.

(Aside)

But, I see Jenny coming. Good God, I hope she doesn't ruin all my good work.

(Enter Jenny)

Jenny

What the Devil are you two doing—are you tied to a stake? Dinner's getting cold, my mistress is annoyed. Ah, there you are, sir. Truly, I am delighted.

McNaughten

What for?

Jenny

I'm sent to see what prevents you from coming. My lady cannot understand the reason. But, what is this, sir, why the mourning outfit and the lugubrious reception? You act as if you didn't know me?

McNaughten

Miss—

Jenny

Why have you gone into mourning so suddenly? Do you think this is the way to dress for a dinner party? Are you coming from a funeral, sir?

McNaughten

What's it to you? I'll dress as I please.

(Low to Spruce)

The girls around here are well equipped with effrontery and curiosity.

Spruce

It's the custom of the town. They're always friendly with people they've never met. Beware a trap.

Jenny

My concern in this matter is natural enough. Whatever happens to you interests me. My lady has an extreme tenderness for you, and I must imitate her.

McNaughten

Quite unnecessary.

Jenny

Sir!

McNaughten

You pretend your mistress loves me, do you?

Jenny

You pretend you don't know that?

McNaughten

May I be hanged if I ever heard of it before this moment!

Jenny (puzzled)

You've had several proofs already. And if you want more solid proof, you can bed her and marry her whenever you like.

McNaughten

I can bed her?

Jenny

Easily.

McNaughten

And marry her?

Jenny

Yes, indeed.

McNaughten

Why would I want to do that?

Jenny

You don't have any other object in view, do you?

McNaughten

The proposition is very straightforward, on my word.

(Aside to Spruce)

On my oath, this wench is a procuress.

Spruce (protesting)

I rather like her that way.

Jenny

Before your return thousands came to offer for her hand, but McNaughten is the only one who ever earned her love.

McNaughten (astounded)

How'd you know my name?

Jenny

How do you know mine?

McNaughten

How do I know YOUR name?

Jenny

Exactly. Same way.

McNaughten

I don't know it at all. Who the Devil are you, anyway?

Jenny

What's the meaning of this joke? My name's Jenny, and I serve Urania. And I've seen you there more than a thousand times.

McNaughten

You're her servant?

Jenny

Now you've got it.

McNaughten

My word! So much the worse for you. I know nothing about it. But, it's really a shame to think such a young girl is engaged in such a sinful school.

Jenny

Quit joking. In one word, my lady is waiting dinner for you. To please you, she's invited her girlfriend, who is pretty and very vivacious.

McNaughten

Your mistress does very good work.

Jenny (to Spruce, giving up on McNaughten)

You talk to me, then? Tell me, what vapor has deranged his mind in so short a time?

Spruce (aside to Jenny)

For some time he's been subject to distractions—the effect of which you can see for yourself. Sometimes, he talks idly and without any sense. He often speaks wildly.

Jenny (to Spruce)

Usually, he seems sensible enough. How can one lose one's memory and reason in such a short time?

(To McNaughten)

Do you intend to speak sensibly to me?

McNaughten

My dear, I am reasonable enough. It's you who are drunk or crazy. Do you intend to bother me with your nonsensical stories for an hour? Who is this Urania who adores me? You talk of dinner, a pretty friend, and a hundred other things, each one more stupid than the other. And which I don't comprehend any more than I do algebra or the Koran.

Jenny

You have no intention of being reasonable or dining with us, as you promised?

McNaughten

The answer is no. I give myself to the Devil—and your mistress, too, with her noble plans. Let other birds fall into her snares. And you, her emissary and honest agent, do you not know it's a villainous thing to be a bawd?

Some evil will befall you. Pray God for forgiveness. Go—and sin no more. I warn you, quit this line of work. Be guided by my advice—it's for your own good.

Jenny

Well! I never have been so insulted in my life. Dare to call me a bawd!

McNaughten

Don't expect to catch me in your traps. I'm no country bumpkin.

Jenny

We will see if you have the nerve to say such stupid things to my lady. Because, I am going to tell her everything you said, and, I won't omit one word. Be sure of it!

(to Spruce)

Goodbye, worthy valet of an unworthy master. I hope after a while we'll know each other better.

(aside)

I don't understand any of it, and I hardly know where I am at!

(Exit Jenny)

McNaughten

My God! What a town. What a strange place. They told me the London women were bold, and that to succeed in their secret practices, they inform themselves about newcomers with great care. But this is unbelievable.

Spruce

She must have heard your name on the stagecoach. She decided to make use of it when you got here, so that she could get something from you.

McNaughten

Right. That's how she knew. But, I defy their plots!

Spruce (slyly)

If you had gone with her, (he gestures of someone being knocked over the head) it might have been all over for you. For both of us, in fact.

McNaughten

Thank God, I know how to protect myself. If they've got it in their head to trick me— Well, it won't work with such beastly tricks as these. I wasn't born yesterday.

Spruce

Better not stay in this place too long. The women of London have lures that force the proudest hearts to succumb.

McNaughten

Your advice is good. Let's go in without lingering.

(Enter Urania and Jenny)

Jenny

You will see if I lie—. Speak to him. There he is!

(Aside)

The lout.

Urania

While I am dying of impatience to see you, you wait here quite indifferent. Dinner is getting cold. You know I have no pleasure except when you are by.

McNaughten

In truth, Madame, I must tell you that I am very surprised—

Spruce (aside)

Be careful, sir. One friendly word might—

McNaughten (aside)

Leave it to me.

(Aloud)

In my surprise— I find it very surprising—your attractions are a little distracting—and confound me. Besides—

My word, I don't know what to say.

Urania

The distraction I see you in suggests you've been involved in some bad business. Why didn't you tell me of this sad event? Tell me, dear child, have you been badly hurt—beaten up? Don't keep anything from me.

McNaughten (pulling himself together)

Never. I haven't been fighting.

Urania

Is it money? All my wealth is yours.— When one loves and when one has only the purest ends in view, all the good and the bad, the pleasures and the pains—everything must be shared equally. I want my fortune to run with yours.

McNaughten (low)

So, that's it. Wants my money.

(Aloud)

I am obliged to you for the sentiment, but I have no need for the kindness you offer me.

Urania

I don't understand this. This isn't the way you usually talk.

Spruce (low)

He's very rude, the way he talks. The better for us.

Urania

Please, let's go in to dinner.

McNaughten (low)

I'll humor her.

(Aloud)

I cannot now. I have some other business.

Urania

I don't want to force you, but I'm frightened by your coldness.

McNaughten (furiously)

What the Devil is this! Leave and finish. I am neither hot nor cold for you.

Jenny

Well! Can he carry this impudence any farther? Stop, sir, you push your insolence too far. My word, if you come to us again, I'm going to slam the door in your face.

Urania

But, where've you been? Stop hiding things from me.

McNaughten

You pretend to be ignorant, Madame, but you know very well. Didn't you see me on the stagecoach? So, you know where I've been and where I'm going. It's your business.

Urania

What a reproach! And what stage are you talking of?

McNaughten

The most vulgar one can go on. I doubt there's another between London and Bristol that better jolts the passengers.

Urania (helplessly)

You're right, he's lost his mind.

Jenny

He hasn't lost a thing. Surely, he's had too much to drink. It's wine that carries him to these extravagances.

McNaughten

I've had enough of your impertinences. More important business calls me away, and it's to finish that business that I am here. To get married, and not to dine with creatures like you who seek adventures.

Urania

Creatures! Adventures! Heavens! What a way to speak to me!

Jenny

Creatures! Ah, Madame, here are two fabulous cheats. If you listen to me, we'll box their ears and avenge our pride.

McNaughten

Softly, if you please. Moderate your passion.

Jenny

I've never felt so wild. I would have spared the valet—but he does nothing to separate himself from his master.

Why, Spruce?

Spruce

I don't wish to know of your differences. I do not want

to fight with you. If he brutalizes you, why blame me?

Urania

How unhappy I am and how weak to have declared my affection for this ingrate! Jenny, you know it—I hide nothing from you.

Jenny

Perfidious wretch—isn't your heart touched?

McNaughten

There, there, take it easy. If this extreme love has come on so swiftly, mark my words, it will soon pass off.

Urania (having made up her mind)

Go!— Expect nothing more from me, but hate and malice.

McNaughten

Fine. I can easily do without your favors.

Jenny

Ah, cursed renegade. Most wicked man in the world. May Heaven punish you and Hell confound you. By rights, we should strangle you.

(Aside)

Surely, he's been bewitched—he just isn't himself.

(Exit Urania and Jenny in great wrath)

McNaughten

Go with God, my princess. Choose more wisely where you form your rapid attachments. But see, what rage, what an outburst of passion. Now I feel a bit sorry, the Devil's tempting me. The maid had an appetizing face.

Spruce (aside)

I'd better stop this.

(Aloud)

You've fought very bravely to the end—and one cannot praise your strength too highly. But beware, they might come back. Who knows what they will try next? So as not to have any more interruptions, let's go into the hotel. Then, if you think me worthy of some employment, you can give me something to do.

McNaughten

I am dying to see the woman I am going to marry. Curiosity, more than love, pushes me on.

Spruce

After you've inspected your room and freshened up, I will gladly escort you to her.

McNaughten

Good—wait until I return.

(Exit McNaughten to the hotel)

Spruce

I am going to find my master to find out what state things are in. He'll look well in mourning. Courage, Spruce, be firm. Steady head, steady hand. I will need all my skill.

CURTAIN

ACT II
SCENE 3

Later that day. The same. Captain McNaughten, dressed in mourning enters, in conversation with Spruce.

Spruce

Nothing is more surprising! Your resemblance to your twin passes belief. You and he are really one. With you both dressed in black, no one can tell the difference. I, your valet, cannot even be sure. So as not to be deceived myself, let me put a mark on you. Give me your hat.

Captain (giving his hat to Spruce)

What do you intend to do?

Spruce (putting a yellow ribbon on the hat)

To put my mark on you, just like your father did, to better distinguish you.

Captain

I think you're trying to make me laugh.

Spruce

I'm not joking. I could very easily make a mistake.

Captain

Mr. Torrington is already quite taken in. He met me right away, was very obliging, and within the hour will pay me my money.

Spruce

What! He's going to pay over the entire inheritance? Sixty thousand pounds.

Captain (airily)

The whole thing.

Spruce

What an honest man. But, let me tell you what has happened. On this very spot, others have taken your twin for you. Urania did so, and so did Jenny. Urania wanted to have him for dinner. He, surprised, not knowing what to say, and taking it to be a trap for his virtue, treated her very rudely, and was almost ready to fight with her. If I hadn't made peace between them, there would have been a mortal battle between man and woman.

Captain

Haven't they suspected the mistake?

Spruce

How can they suspect you? For twenty years, they've thought you dead, and never, no matter how hard they try, can they figure the situation out.

Captain

It's a pleasant adventure, and keeps me in good humor. But look—my father-in-law's coming. Let's carry on the sport. Accost him immediately.

(Enter Sir George Hastings)

Spruce

Sir, are you an honest man by the name of Hastings?

Hastings

That's my name.

Spruce

Delighted to meet you. Here is my master, freshly

arrived, named McNaughten, coming from Scotland, just to marry your daughter.

Hastings

Ah, sir, hopefully this unexpected meeting will show you how glad I am you are here.

Captain

And you, too, sir, witness a parallel joy and respect in your intended son-in-law.

Hastings

Your figure, your air, your wit—enchant me. My heart would be completely happy if your late uncle, whom I met with often to conclude this marriage, was still alive.

Captain

Ah, sir, don't recall his death. An uncle that I loved with a tender regard. This boy can tell you of my excessive sorrow, and how, at his death, I was awash in tears.

Spruce

How Heaven made his soul miserable! But to speak of him is to touch a very tender nerve and might— But he was very old.

Hastings

Not so very old, same age with me, about fifty.

Spruce

The word old can be understood in many ways. I speak of old with respect to his health. He was always complaining of some infirmity.

Hastings

Not at all. He was never attacked by a malady in his entire life until the horrible accident which caused his death.

Captain

He had an iron constitution.

Spruce (aside to Captain)

Now, you're right.

Captain (aside to Spruce)

Shut up, then.

Hastings

This conversation will awaken your grief. Let's talk of something more lively and gay. You are going to see my daughter, and I flatter myself you will be very content with her looks and her vivacity.

Captain

I hope that duty will answer for me. I count very little on my own will.

Hastings

You are quite wrong. Rely on enchanting her at first sight. I know women, and, take my word, Flavella is a wax tablet which I mold and form to my pleasure. I'll be very much surprised if you are not to her taste. I am her father, and to show you how much she defers to my wishes, just step aside. I am going to call her, and, without her seeing you, you will see how she responds to you.

(Exit Hastings)

Captain

Leave me here. Go find my brother. The main thing is to prevent him from meeting Mr. Torrington. Make sure!

Spruce

I agree. But, in the romantic mood he's in, I don't guarantee I'll be able to prevent him from seeing Miss Flavella.

So, press her ardently, but be quick about it, there's no time to waste.

Captain

Go, quickly. I won't lose any time here. (steps aside)

(Exit Spruce in one direction. From another, enter Hastings and Flavella.)

Hastings

Now, come along, Flavella.

Flavella

What is it, father?

Hastings

To be brief about it, a man from Scotland has just arrived. He's very good-looking, and he's here to marry you.

Flavella (aside)

What do I hear?

Hastings

It's a perfect match—birth, wealth, family, all to my taste, and, as to his person—his person will suit you, my dear, suit you perfectly.

Flavella

Father, without, without pushing this conversation any further, permit me to say, with deference and without showing any lack of obedience—I HAVE NO INTENTION OF GETTING MARRIED!

Hastings

What? When did you decide that? You never used to talk like this.

Flavella

True, but wisdom comes with age. I know the danger now. Today husbands are, for the most part, jealous and unfaithful. They want a woman to marry their caprices. The best husbands are those with only a FEW vices.

Hastings

But, he's a very nice, young man. You'll like him when you get to know him.

Flavella

I ALREADY HATE HIM WITHOUT SEEING HIM! It's enough that he's a Scotsman and wears kilts. I wouldn't have him if he were a prince.

Captain (appearing)

Madame, it's not necessary to be so passionate against the poor unfortunate your father wants to give you. If you hate him, he can find others whose sentiments differ from yours.

Flavella (aside)

Good Heavens, what do I see! How astonishing! It's Captain McNaughten, dear God, it's my lover.

Hastings

I am in despair that such a distaste has rendered her spirit so contrary to my wishes. But, I will force her, if you wish me to—

Captain

No, sir, do not force her inclinations. I would rather die than constrain Madame's heart.

Hastings

Look him over, daughter. He's a husband practically made to order. He's a young man, well-born, and his spirit is the equal of his birth and wealth.

Captain (plaintively)

I was wrong to set my hopes so high.

Flavella

What—is this the man you propose for me?

Hastings

Yes—if you don't cross me in my choice. If your stupid, crazy ideas don't ruin all my plans and care.

Flavella

To be honest with you, after seeing him, my heart isn't so set against marriage as it was before.

Captain

You have such a passionate hate for me—can your eye accustom itself to look on me?

Flavella

My father's the boss. I will do everything daddy says.

(Enter Urania)

Urania

Ah, you are still here, traitor! With what impudence do you dare to remain in my presence, after you have treated me with such indignity? Aren't you afraid of my just anger?

Captain

Madame, I don't know what you are trying to say, and this brusque conversation bewilders me. You mistake me for someone else, I am sure. What complaint have you against me?

Urania

Two-faced traitor! Do you pretend not to know me? You tricked me with a pretended passion, and I, in good faith—I gave you my heart—

(wailing)—without knowing yours and all its darkness!

Captain

You honor me with all my defects, but truly, I don't understand a word you are talking about.

Hastings

My word, neither do I. But tell me, sister, what are you getting at? This bizarre humor—

Captain

This lady is your sister?

Hastings

Yes, sir—who infuriates me—my elder sister, but not wiser. What new caprice, what new demon, I say, makes you come play mischief? To scandalize this poor gentleman who never saw you before in his life? How could he have harmed you, a perfect stranger?

Urania

Doesn't know me! A perfect stranger! I believe you're mad. For two years, this ingrate has been my suitor—my lover. This gigolo has drawn on my wealth, and I have paid for practically every thing he wears. If I hadn't taken pity on his misfortunes, he would long ago have been on the dole.

Hastings

I told you so; she's a little crazy.

Captain

Still, she seems normal. Some sort of mistake.

Hastings

Oh, I give you my word.

Captain

In any event, I don't relish lingering here any longer to

listen to this insulting discourse. I leave the battle field to the lady. I will return as soon as she leaves.

Hastings

No one can stop her from talking. You have to put up with her difficult nature.

Captain

For a while, sir, permit me to leave you. I will return to finish my visit.

(Exit Captain)

Urania (pursuing him part way)

Don't think to escape me. I know your plans. You may try to tear him from my arms, but I swear I will marry him, in spite of the daughter, the father, the relations, the whole family—in spite of him, and in spite of myself, too.

(Exit Urania after the Captain)

Hastings

What vertigo disturbs her and brings her here? As she gets older, her head seems to get more and more disturbed.

Flavella

It's true. I'm very often ashamed for her.

Hastings

I am afraid that this woman, with her unaccountable temper, may come here and cause some misfortune.

(Enter McNaughten and Spruce)

Spruce (to McNaughten)

Yes, sir, here they are: the father and daughter, together. You can speak with both of them about your affair.

Hastings

Ah, sir, my daughter and I must beg your pardon for my sister and her wild delusions. You conceive, sir, that women, like little girls, sometimes have spirits that go against their family.

McNaughten

Ah—yes—sir.

Hastings

You return quickly. I am delighted.

McNaughten

I come to wish you a good day. And, at the same time, to marry a lady named Flavella, whose father you are—at least everyone says so. In short, that is what brings me here.

Hastings

I've already told you, and I repeat, how much this pleases me. My daughter is happy, too. Having seen you, she now submits to love and duty. At first, she had a slight distaste—but after seeing you, her heart melted.

McNaughten (puzzled)

We've met before?

Hastings

Just now. You left her here, and appeared content.

McNaughten

Me? I left her here?

Hastings

YOU, without a doubt. Certainly. We were just greeting you, with great joy, when my sister came with her crazy talk, and interrupted our conversation. How can you forget so soon?

McNaughten

Someone is dreaming—either you or me! What! You would have me believe that I have already seen your daughter! When? How? Where?

Hastings

Right here—on this spot—a little while ago.

McNaughten

So, you're crazy. This will make me look like a person having hallucinations, and I don't like that at all. However that may be, I see her now. Whether it is the first or second time makes little difference for our marriage.

Hastings (low)

At first I thought this man was very intelligent.

McNaughten

Madame, they've boasted to me, in letters, about your attractions. I'm quite content, seeing you, that all that was true. But, in some cases, temperament doesn't go together with beauty. It's up to you to cure my apprehensions on that score. I will give my verdict, after you have spoken.

Flavella (aside)

I don't understand him. His mind is troubled.

McNaughten

I love men of spirit more than any man in England. I, myself, am brilliant without study. I find that study is the perfect way to spoil one's youth—besides being no use whatever. So, I've never stuck my nose in a book. When a gentleman knows how to ride and steer his horse, drink, sign his name, he is as wise a gentleman as the late Cicero.

Hastings

Will you take a position at court or in the Army?

McNaughten

My mind is not made up. Court has many powerful attractions—provided the routine doesn't fatigue me. War also has its attractions. Because savants versed in astrology have assured me that I will live to be at least a hundred, necessarily I will not die on the battlefield. My name will be famous throughout Europe. But still, there are so few wars these days. I really want to fulfill my destiny. If I only knew what it was. I really love to live.

Spruce

You are very wise.

Flavella

What a speech! What nonsense! Am I really listening to the man I love?

McNaughten

What's wrong? You appear surprised—as if I'd said something crazy. You look to me—

(addressing Flavella)—let's speak openly—as if you have little intention of heeding any lesson from your husband.

Flavella (icily)

I know what my duty is as an engaged woman.

McNaughten

To be sure, I think you are virtuous and prudent. But you've got an amorous and sly look about you that doesn't augur well for me in the future. Without being a fortune-teller, I predict you are planning some little trick to play on me in the future. True? What do you say?

Hastings

Sir, fear nothing. My daughter always behaves herself properly.

McNaughten

The sly ones always behave with great propriety.

Flavella

Heavens! Can he say this to my face? Father, let me leave. This gentleman flatters me too much. His tender compliments allow me to understand his sentiments only too well.

(Exit Flavella before her father can reply)

Hastings (aside)

I thought at first my son-in-law had beautiful manners.

McNaughten

Women don't really like sincerity very much.

Spruce

You don't flatter them.

McNaughten

By God, I am frank. Woman, mistress, friend, are all alike to me. I am not afraid to say what I think.

Hastings

That's very proper. Everything will be fine. Please stay at my house.

McNaughten

I receive that gracious offer in the proper spirit, but—

Hastings

To let you suffer in a hotel would be an insult.

McNaughten

I beg you to let me stay at liberty a little longer.

Hastings

So be it! I am going to see about this marriage contract.

(Aside)

My would-be son-in-law appears a savage. But his wealth redeems all.

(Exit Hastings)

McNaughten (slowly)

I have seen the object I am to marry.

Spruce

Yes, sir. Right here.

McNaughten

Tell me, frankly, what do you think?

Spruce

To be honest with you, I didn't find many perfections.

McNaughten

My word, neither did I.

Spruce (aside)

What an additional embarrassment. One of our creditors is bearing down on us. It's the old clothes merchant who is paying us a visit.

(Enter Mr. Bronlow)

Bronlow (greeting McNaughten)

My humble duties. I learned this morning of your return, sir. I have come to be the first to welcome you to England. We were all worried about you. Extremely worried, I may say. In my establishment, everybody loves you, me, my daughter, my wife—we all tremble with fear that something might happen to you.

McNaughten

Such good souls to love me without having seen me! I never would have believed it.

Bronlow

We owe it to you, sir. And for very good reason. You've been a friend of our house for a very long time.

McNaughten (to Spruce, low)

Who is this man?

Spruce (low)

He's—he's a visionary. A type of lunatic—with a pleasant character—

(making it up as he goes along, and becoming more and more inspired)—who believes everyone he meets owes him money. It's his folly to greet everyone he meets and present them with a promissory note—and to demand payment. I am surprised that he hasn't paid you the compliment already.

(Aside)

I think I did that rather well.

McNaughten

His madness is novel and rare, assuredly.

Spruce (low, to McNaughten)

It happens all the time in this city. If you stay here long enough, he may not be the only one you meet.

Bronlow

I am delighted to see you in such good health. More than you can imagine. Here's a little bill you ran up before you left. I am sure you won't quibble about paying it.

Spruce (triumphantly)

What did I tell you!

Bronlow

Because you were away so long, I was obliged to sue out a judgment against you.

McNaughten

A personal judgment against me!

Bronlow

But, kindly creditor that I am—I differ extremely from process servers whose suits and writs give people headaches—I present the bill myself—

McNaughten

You're truly very good and honest. What might be your name?

Bronlow

Oh—you know it very well.

McNaughten

Let me be hanged if I know it at all!

Bronlow

Could you possibly forget?

Spruce (aside to Bronlow)

Are you unable to see the illness he's suffering from?

Bronlow

Indeed, I am unable to see it!

Spruce

He's suffering from amnesia and cannot recall a thing. Neither what he's done nor the people he's seen. Talking to him about the past is not only useless but crazy. His name itself, his very own name, he sometimes forgets!

Bronlow

Heavens, what are you telling me? What a sad event. But how could he, at his young age?

Spruce

How? (puzzled momentarily) How? He lost it in the war—in a battery with the cannon roaring with such fury that it made a commotion in his head—which prevents him from remembering anything. In his weak head—this tender membrane. Oh, you cannot understand the effect of a cannon.

Bronlow (very decently)

I am terribly sorry for what has befallen you, but I assure you that you do owe me this money.

McNaughten

I can see very clearly that reason has taken leave of you.

Bronlow

Sir, try to recall those uniforms I supplied you with.

McNaughten

Uniforms to me! Go collect your imaginary bills elsewhere. I haven't the time to listen to your nonsense. You are an old fool.

Bronlow

I am a clothes merchant. My name is Bronlow Incorporated, and I am a churchwarden. If you've lost your memory, the articles are listed in the bill of sale, which if you would kindly read, will inform you—

(Presenting a bill of sale to McNaughten)

McNaughten (tearing it up and throwing the pieces in Bronlow's face)

Here, take your foolish bill of sale! I've done with it.

Spruce (to Bronlow, who is horrified)

Oh, sir, against a madman, it is useless to contend.

Bronlow (gathering up the pieces)

To tear up a bill of sale; to throw it in my face. You are a cheater!

McNaughten (ready to attack Bronlow)

Me? A cheater?

Spruce (putting himself between them)

Gentlemen—please—

Bronlow

I will show you.

Spruce (to Bronlow)

Not so much noise. Consider the state to which he has been reduced.

Bronlow

To tear up a receipt!

Spruce

Not such a big thing.

Bronlow

It's a frightful crime—worthy of transportation.

McNaughten

Let me pull his ears!

Spruce

Leave him alone. What would you do to a poor church-warden?

(To Bronlow)

If you argue any more something terrible may happen.

Bronlow

I want to be paid. I don't give a damn about the rest.

Spruce (to Bronlow)

Leave, sir, leave. Do you want to rekindle the flames in his overheated mind with your screaming?

Bronlow

Very well—I will leave. But before an hour has passed, I am going to make him change his tune. Your humble servant.

(Exit Mr. Bronlow)

Spruce

What's the use of getting irritated by a madman?

McNaughten

What? Does he seek me out to be the butt of his impertinences? Let him take his extravagances down another road. Let's go to Mr. Torrington without waiting any further.

Spruce

Presently, Sir—now it would be a wasted effort. He isn't home, but he'll be back soon. In a little while, I'll return and take you to see him. A certain pressing duty calls me away suddenly.

McNaughten

I will wait for you. Go, but don't delay. I need to calm down. I begin to believe everyone in this city is crazy. Of all the people I've met today, I've only found one. besides myself, who is reasonable, and that's you.

(Exit McNaughten to the hotel)

Spruce

I intend to inspect everything. Let's see. The fish himself is in our net. Everything is going according to plan.

Today, I serve two gods— Fortune and Cupid. I hope to make myself useful!

BLACKOUT

ACT II
SCENE 4

The same, a short while later. Spruce is standing in front of the hotel.

Spruce

I've been watching this door, and no one has come out. My master has had time to get his money and run. And I, diligent accomplice that I am, wait here to make sure that the brother doesn't spoil things by running to Torrington and discovering this mystery. Already, a creditor has embarrassed me. It's laughable to think all that's happened.

I've put things into the hands of a man with an ardent imagination. God, if McNaughten were a bit less headstrong and argumentative, he'd have seen through it all by now. Thank Heaven for passionate people. But I see Jenny coming. My amorous heart ignites with new flames in her presence.

(Enter Jenny)

Jenny

I am come to look for your master.

Spruce

While waiting for him to come, permit my love to entertain you. Let me sacrifice my heart at the altar of your matchless charms.

Jenny

Take your sacrifices elsewhere, and never trouble yourself to speak to me again! Your master has treated me with disrespect, and I am going to be avenged on you for it. To call me a creature!

Spruce

But, is that my fault?

Jenny (implacably)

You are his valet!

Spruce

Ha, don't pay attention to him. Sometimes, he's like that. Hard and brutal as a dog.

Jenny

My ears are still ringing from his villainous words, and, my lady is so scandalized that she is breaking with him, forever, even though it breaks her poor heart. I am sent to collect her portrait and all her letters.

Spruce

It's useless to keep the letters, but as to the portrait—the frame is made of gold and studded with diamonds. It's my considered opinion that he should not part with the portrait—it's too precious to give back—from sentiment, of course. The two are not the same. We can pawn it, if the need for money drives us to extremities, my child.

Jenny

Why make such a big fuss over a portrait?

Spruce

Because, we were in big trouble not long ago. Once burned, twice shy. Fortunately, an uncle—a very honest man, has helped us out, by voluntarily descending to the underworld quicker than we could say his name. He has saved us in a very timely fashion, by making us heirs to sixty thousand pounds.

Jenny

Ah, Heavens, so that's it!

Spruce

I tell you the truth.

Jenny

So—in such a short time, you've become rich.

Spruce

Right! We've received the sad but happy news of his death and the princely bequest, and have got our money in less time than it takes to tell you of it. My master is devilishly close to success.

Jenny

Oh, I don't doubt it.

Spruce

Judge for yourself. You see, he would have done a very foolish thing to remain faithful to your lady under the circumstances. One must trim one's sail to the wind.

Jenny

The world is full of lovers like that.

Spruce

Following his example, I am quitting the shop girls and the scullery maids. My love wishes to rise to hearts of a higher rank. I will take proud flight and rise to the peaks. The money will pass through my trusty hands, and, fortunately, they're sticky. I believe I will throw myself into business.

Jenny

You are going into business? You!

Spruce

Before two years have passed, watch me go by in a magnificent chaise—on my way to the country. I'll be burning the paving stones with the gallop of six Spanish horses. A French barber, numerous valets, countless attendants, cooks—and pretty chambermaids will fill my palace. My buffet will be of gold and porcelain. The wine will flow like water in the Thames. My table will be open, my days, libertine. When I wish to give a secret little supper, I will have a cozy retreat prepared, where I will feast the fair ladies. One day, this one; the next, that one. And I promise you, when your turn comes, and even before that, to treat you to a feast.

Jenny (sarcastically)

I am overwhelmed!

Spruce

For you, my tenderness knows no bounds. But, look who's coming. It's McNaughten himself. At your command, sir. You see me prepared to do my duty.

(Enter McNaughten)

McNaughten

You've waited for me in this place for some time. Meanwhile, I've found a paper that will expedite our little business with Mr. Torrington.

Jenny

My mistress has decided to break with you forever. She has sent me here to collect her portrait, her letters, her jewels, and everything that belongs to her. She has ordered me to return to you, yours. Here they are.

(giving him a packet of letters and a portrait)

McNaughten (stunned)

All this, here, has been with her for a long time?

Jenny

It's the custom amongst HONEST people, when they quarrel and make a final break, to return each other's letters and portraits.

McNaughten

Is it so?

Jenny

Yes, sir—without fail. This young man here will tell you so. Those who live properly pride themselves on it.

McNaughten

Look here, my dear, all of this is a terrible nuisance, and you should realize that I'm getting tired of putting up with it.

Jenny

Stop playing around! Here's your portrait—now give me hers, and, I'll be off!

McNaughten

My portrait—what are you talking about?

Jenny

Yes, your portrait, which my mistress exchanged for hers—bad bargain, though it was.

McNaughten (feebly)

I gave MY portrait to YOUR mistress?

Jenny

Look, are you going to pretend this is all a fable? That it is all false?

McNaughten

Why, yes, by all the Devils, that is what I say, and what I will maintain, now and forever.

Jenny

Surely, you wouldn't dare to take your oath on that, sir?

McNaughten

Yes, I swear it. For, I've never had my portrait drawn, which proves it beyond question.

Spruce

This is no time to feign. If you have received it, no matter how—you are going too far.

McNaughten

I don't know anything about it—may the Devil take me if I do!

Jenny

Isn't this your portrait in this locket?

McNaughten

No—unless the Devil, to injure me, painted it with his own hands and gave it to you.

Jenny

What audacity—what effrontery! But, I will confound you. Look—what can you say to this witness?

(opening the locket) Well—do you know the face and the features?

McNaughten

How the Devil! It's—me. Who'd ever have thought such a thing possible? Those are my eyes, my look.

Spruce (taking the portrait from Jenny)

Let's have a look, please. Put the original beside the copy. My word—it is you, all right. A speaking portrait. Never did a painter draw a better likeness.

McNaughten

There's some sorcery—or at least some trick. You will see. These two creatures painted it while I was on the coach—just to play me some trick. It's all part of their plan.

Jenny

Stop it, please.

McNaughten

Stop it yourself! Go try to meet men some other way, and leave me alone.

Jenny

Give me back the portrait!

McNaughten

Of whom?

Jenny

Of my mistress, who else?

McNaughten (grabbing her roughly by the shoulders)

I don't know anything about it. Get out and leave me alone.

Jenny

Do you know, sir, that before leaving this place, I am going to scratch your eyes out?

Spruce

Sir, to avoid any further quarrel—give her her portrait. You know a woman scorned is a hundred times more vicious than all the Devils in Hell.

McNaughten

But, were she a thousand times more of a Devil than she is—I don't know her or her mistress.

Spruce (to Jenny)

Never mind what he says. He must still be in love with her. Let me soften him up a bit. Come back soon, and I will have it for you.

Jenny

Oh, all right. I can wait a little. But if he refuses to listen to reason when I get back, I am going to burn the house down, understand?

(Smiling)

(Exit Jenny)

McNaughten

I don't know which of those harridans is more frightening: the mistress or the maid. How can perfect strangers be so enthusiastic about persecuting me—?

Like furies from Hell.

Spruce

A man like you—young, loveable, handsome—is subject to these misfortunes. Between lovers, fights like these are mere bagatelles. From today, I promise to make you friends with her.

McNaughten

Lord forbid.

Spruce (aside)

But, who do I see coming this way? It's the Squire. That hundred pounds is going to spell trouble for us.

(Enter the Squire)

Squire

Hey, dear fellow, what luck—let me embrace you a thousand times to show you how happy I am to see you.

Look at me—I was outré—in despair. This has been a horrible day, I've had nothing but bad luck until—Lo! I meet you. I've been buffeted on all sides by fate. Just like a football.

McNaughten

Sir, I am sorry to see you this way, but I have no time to struggle with you.

Squire

A pistol shot would be good for me. I wish someone would crush me into the ground.

McNaughten

Who is this Irishman?

Spruce

Evidently, a dear friend of yours—although I think he's Welsh.

McNaughten

I've never seen him before.

Squire

I've just left a house—may the earth swallow it, and nature perish with it—where I lost my last penny at cards.

Outrageous luck. So, I am obliged to ask you for the hundred pounds I loaned you when you were in need. Excuse my importuning you, but you will pardon me—you can see what a state I am in.

McNaughten

I pardon you, entirely, and you will pardon me, too, if I say that this surprises me entirely. I don't know you. How could you lend me a hundred pounds, never having seen me before?

Squire (coldly)

What kind of talk is this? It passes my understanding.

McNaughten

I suppose your talk is easier to comprehend?

Squire

You pretend you don't owe me a hundred pounds?

McNaughten

No—on my oath. You've loaned to someone else, not me.

Squire

Perhaps, you don't recall, that before going to Germany, you needed money for the campaign—not having enough money to buy a mule, let alone a horse—

McNaughten

I don't recall a word of all this. I've never been to Germany.

Squire

That's where you said you were going. You came to me for help, and I opened my purse for you, without any uncalled for remarks.

McNaughten

To me? I'd have to be crazy to borrow money from a Scotsman, or Irishman, or whatever you are.

Squire (icily)

Sir, I am Welsh. This man here can bear witness; he was with you—I recall his face. Come here, boy. Speak! Do you dare deny what his evil heart tries in vain to forget?

Spruce (terrified)

Sir—

Squire

Speak, or my hand, possessed by fury, will—

Spruce

It comes to me in a confused way—

Squire

A confused way. Well, I am certain of it. I see you are no better than your master. Though I blame you less— perhaps you fear your place or a beating.

(To McNaughten)

Now, sir, give me my money, or take your sword.

McNaughten

What! Because I refuse to give you a hundred pounds, you compel me to fight!

Squire

A little. Breaking an oath puts me in temper. Quickly— defend yourself.

McNaughten

I am in no great rush. Let's discuss it further.

Squire

No discussion. Your choice is clear.

McNaughten

But, sir—

Squire

But, sir— You must give me satisfaction

McNaughten

Me, give you, satisfaction? But, I swear, I don't owe you a penny. Sue me—I will respond in court.

Squire

You know, very well, I did not even ask for a receipt! When someone owes me—I carry my own bailiff.

(drawing his sword)

McNaughten

Just Heaven—the brute! How am I to get out of this, without being maimed or killed? How much do you insist I owe you?

Squire

A hundred pounds. How easily you forget.

McNaughten

But, I can't pay you a hundred pounds. I will give you half.

Squire

May I be pulverized to atoms, you will pay me my hundred pounds in a quarter of an hour or I will kill you instantly.

Spruce (low to McNaughten)

The villain is prepared to kill us both, I believe. Give it to him—if you're dead, what good will the sixty thousand pounds do you? Answer him softly. The man is desperate and has nothing to lose.

McNaughten

But, it's robbery.

Spruce

Exactly. Your money or our lives.

McNaughten

He's very rude and I don't like him.

Spruce

What a time for reflections.

McNaughten

If you are in such a hurry, sir, so much the worse for you. I'll seek another time to be angry. I haven't got a hundred pounds, but here are sixty.

(To Spruce)

Give it to him, to calm him.

(Aside)

Ah, if I were not in line for this sixty thousand pounds, I would die fighting, before I gave him a farthing. He looks formidable, though. It would be quite a skirmish.

Spruce

Here's more than half your debt, sir. Tomorrow, you will have the entire amount.

McNaughten

I want it clearly understood, that I protest, I do not owe you a penny. I am paying you only because you insist that I do.

Squire (taking the purse)

Goodday, sir, goodday. I see your soul. You spoke of honor to me, but this proves the contrary. Never come near me again. No more of this business. My nobility would be degraded in the presence of a coward like you.

(Exit Squire)

McNaughten

Ha, has he got a nerve, to talk like that? Where am I? In what country? Can this be England? What a race of perjurers. Men, women, squires, merchants, customs officers, Welshmen. They all seem united in an effort to enrage me. I don't know one of them, and they all pretend to be my best friend come to surprise me. Let's go to Torrington and get out of this frightful situation.

(McNaughten starts to leave)

Spruce (running after him and catching him)

Don't you want me to escort you to him?

McNaughten

I have no further need of your help. I am obliged to you for the services you have rendered.

(giving him some money) I couldn't praise them more.

But, from now on, I am so extremely suspicious that I am going to fend for myself. Then, I will have only myself to blame if something further goes wrong.

(Exit McNaughten)

Spruce

That fellow has got all his wits about him. He must decamp or go mad. Still, if he stays a bit longer, he'll end up paying off all my master's creditors.

(Enter the Captain)

Captain

Ah, my beloved Spruce, you see me beside myself. My fortune is so great that I can hardly believe it. I have got the money—look! It has force and power. All portable. Bills of Exchange—the best in London. I will purchase two or three titles—with the best estates in England.

Spruce

What a windfall! Wealth comes to you from all sides. Please, let me look over the notes. Beautiful engraving, excellent workmanship. Pretty names. Superb style. Freely negotiable—not like love letters on cheap paper where love distills itself in faded oaths, and idle nonsense.

Captain

I know their worth better than you. But, just as the money did little for me in the past, I hope, in the future, that it will serve me the same way it does others.

Spruce

You don't know how luck has favored you. Your brother was just here, and the Squire who loaned you a hundred pounds suddenly appeared, asking for the money. Your brother, naturally enough, thought the man was insane.

But the Squire, tiring of excuses, drew his sword on the spot. Your twin didn't care to fight—prudently, in my opinion, for that Squire is the very Devil when his Welsh blood is up. So, your brother gave half of it to the Squire, who took it as a reduction,

Captain

I am obliged to him for paying my debts.

Spruce

You don't owe him too much. He's done you a lot of harm with Flavella!

Captain (concerned)

He's seen her?

Spruce

Oh, indeed. He's a little brutal. He satirized her and said some things that would put any woman's dander up. And, of course, she took it as coming from you. Flavella left, rather incensed.

Captain

I've got to undeceive her of this error. But I see her coming. Where are you heading, Madame? Where are you off to?

(Enter Flavella)

Flavella

Someplace you are not.

Spruce

There's tit for tat.

Flavella

I am going to Urania's to tell her she may have you. Love her, I consent. I give her to you. I vow, henceforth, to flee you like a monster and never see you more.

Captain

Madame—

Flavella

In return for the most intense love, what do I receive from you? Insult and invective! It seems I appear to you without honor, wit, or attraction.

Captain

Madame, listen to me—

Flavella

Never. I don't understand how it is possible to be so brutal or to have the audacity, the cold blood, to say such hard things to my very face.

Captain

You know that in a public place—

Flavella

I don't know a thing.

Captain

Everything's all right—

Spruce

Listen, without so much passion.

Flavella

Do you intend that I expose myself again to his stupidities?

Spruce

My Lord, no. You jump to conclusions. In one moment, I am going to dispel all these clouds and prove that you are both wrong (Flavella and the Captain protest) and both right.

Flavella

Yes, I'm certainly right, as even you, can see.

Captain

And I am not wrong.

Spruce

All this little squabbling excites you. In two words it will be all over. The gentleman has said certain harsh words to you?

Flavella

Past all belief.

Captain

But I say—

Spruce

Peace—away with petulance. I won't talk to either of you, if you are always going to interrupt. The man who made this impertinent speech to you is him—except he's not him. It's only his figure, manner, name, and face.

The one looks like the other. But, they differ, both are not the same, and, in fact, are two! Thus, the other one is him—dressed in his skin, the portrait of my Captain— he's the one who spoke so unfeelingly to you.

Flavella

With what kind of nonsense do you hope to confuse me?

Captain

Don't go off without listening to him speak.

Spruce

Maybe I am not making myself clear. Monsieur has a brother in these parts, a twin brother—identical in features and clothes. It was his tongue that lashed you. You took him for this one, who is like him. The other one is a brutal imposter. Here is the real McNaughten.

Flavella

What a strange story. Strange, I haven't heard it before. But—I choose to believe it, as it flatters my pride. Love renders my scorn just and pardonable.

Captain

Your anger renders you more adorable in my eyes. Permit my passion—

(Trying to kiss her)

Flavella

Moderate your passions—

Captain

I am at fault. Too transported by pleasure, I push my passion a little too far. But let us both forget our scorn.

Spruce (showing the Captain's hat)

So as not to be deceived—look for this mark. In a tight spot, it will serve you like a beacon. Know which is which before you make for the justice of the peace to be married.

Flavella

My heart will tell me sooner than my eyes.

Captain

May Heaven today complete my fortune. Without you, I want nothing and renounce everything.

Spruce

Stop the compliments. When you are married, you will have leisure to do that. Remember, Urania is against you.

Let Madame return home in peace for the moment. We must run to make the marriage contract. For now we are at the beginning of the end—or is it the end of the beginning? Anyway, we must finish.

CURTAIN

ACT III
SCENE 5

The street again. Sometime later. Enter Jenny and Urania.

Jenny

I tell you truly, Madame, I don't believe you can find another man with such an evil heart. When I pressed him to return your portrait, he wanted to beat me. And, I believe he would have, if his valet, a man of softer disposition, hadn't diverted his rage. Oh, M'am, arm yourself with courage—follow your point, and be valiant. Pursue your rights. You have him in your power. You have his promise in writing. He'll have to make good on it.

Urania

If I don't make him, let Heaven punish me.

Jenny

Here there is no relying on oaths, on probity. Despite

law and honor, women these days are often trapped. They rely on words, and are deceived. So, to protect ourselves, we must make them put their fair words in writing. It's only fair. But, what use will it be to get it in writing, if we don't enforce the contract? I see very plainly, that in this ungrateful century, one cannot hope to rely on anything that's not in writing. But, we prefer to be the sport and dupes of men.

Urania

Say no more, Jenny. My incensed heart is resolved. If I can, I will avenge our whole sex on this man.

Jenny

What, then? To get the world's attention, does it take more than to wear a pretty wig? An empty head, a little whipper-snapper, who admires only himself, and chatters pleasantly, because he has good manners, can plead with us about his love with complete impunity. He surprises us and makes his ardent declaration—but recoils when it comes time to make good on it. It's a hideous thing that cries to heaven for vengeance. Abuse like this is grounds for revoking the license we give men. Even if you don't want to marry him to avenge yourself, you must do it to enrage him, and to satisfy the rest of us!

Urania (sighing)

But, if he no longer loves me, what good is it to force him into such a sad marriage?

Jenny

Who marries only for love nowadays? That was fine, when you were an adolescent. It's no crime to marry without love, and, even without respect. What's necessary is to marry! You are at an age when your attractions will wither and disappear. The advice I'm giving you, in my zeal, is good. I intend to apply it to myself. To be an old maid is a frightful evil, far worse than all the unhappiness that marriage can cause.

(Enter Hastings and Flavella)

Hastings

Chance has led you here and saved me the trouble of finding you.

Urania

Chance has favored us equally, for I have been saved the trouble of hunting you up.

Hastings

Always preoccupied? Aren't you yet undeceived? Don't you— Don't you realize that your passion is a chimera and a hallucination? Give it up—believe me. You won't profit by crossing my plans. Show yourself to be wise.

Urania

As usual, you babble without rhyme or reason. But, you know what I want to talk about. Here is McNaughten's written promise to marry me; given as a mark of his affection and in his own handwriting.

(Flavella flinches)

Hastings

Where is your credulity leading you, sis?

Urania

He wrote me, I tell you. I've been swindled. Listen, niece—

Flavella

You may be quite sure I'm listening very carefully, auntie.

Urania

Without exaggeration, you are very pleasant to try to steal a heart like his from me, and to appropriate my treasure so boldly. Such an action is stupid and not honest.

Flavella

Who could possibly ravish a conquest from your arms? Your eyes guarantee that when one has been struck by your manifold attraction, they will never change. They are charming eyes which steal men from others.

Urania

My eyes are prettier than yours. We will see who succeeds best if we employ them at the same time!

Hastings

Oh, I am at the end of my patience listening to you both. Happily, I see my son-in-law coming.

(To McNaughten)

Are you bring the solicitor with you?

(Enter McNaughten)

McNaughten

I've been looking for him for nearly an hour, in vain. I finally came to ask you to conduct me to him. Something irritating is always happening to me today.

Hastings

I am waiting for him. I believe he won't be late.

McNaughten

One, after running after me, like one of my most cherished and faithful friends, asked news of my health.

Another forcefully grabbed my hand, and wanted to lead me to a tavern for supper. Then, a third, stopping me in the street, forced me to pay a debt I know nothing about. All these people confound me to Hell! As if I knew them any better than Lucifer!

Urania

Traitor! Are you finished? In spite of your promised word, you intend to marry another? In spite of all your oaths, in spite of your first choice?

McNaughten

Ah, are we still at that?

Urania

You desert me, ingrate, faithless heart. You take pleasure in the cruel pain I suffer. You see me dying and giving in to my fate without shedding one single tear for my death.

(collapsing on Jenny)

McNaughten

This woman is a torment; she must have been bewitched. Must I always have a fury attached to my steps?

Jenny

Can you see my lady expire in my arms? You, who once had so much tenderness for her? This poor innocent—does she deserve to have her love repaid by such cruelty?

McNaughten

Let her expire in your arms. Let the Devil take her, and you with her. Who cares! Already, for my peace and quiet, he might have done that.

Urania (springing back to life)

Perjurer! I will avenge myself for your breach of contract. I have your promise. There's your signature. I have proof of your imposture.

McNaughten (to Hastings)

She's crazier than it's possible to explain. Try, as soon as you can, to have her shut up.

Hastings (reading the contract)

But here's your name: McNaughten. Have you been with her in some way? She is my sister: maybe I can smooth things over.

McNaughten

Me! If I've ever seen those two cheats standing there before today. Pardon the harsh word, one of them is your sister. Never mind. I swear before you, that Satan—Lucifer—

Hastings

I believe you without swearing.

McNaughten

This woman has vowed to make me insane. Spirit, demon, mischief-making witch, woman or fury—whatever you are: I beg you, leave me alone.

(Enter Torrington)

Hastings

Ah, Mr. Torrington, you come just in time, and we await you eagerly.

Torrington

I meet the company with pleasure, reunited on a joyful day in one place. I believe my presence won't displease.

The future has great attractions. Your daughter was only lacking a husband—despite all her attractions, she was incomplete. But, now, behold the well-made man love has given her. Now, she has nothing to desire.

McNaughten

Except to be a widow, and see me buried. That is the finishing touch on the happiness of a woman.

Flavella

Such ideas never entered my mind.

Torrington (laughing uneasily)

The gentleman says what he thinks. Your beauty charms him as much as your wit. I promise you, he's an honest man. I vouch for him.

McNaughten

You're joking, sir.

Torrington

And, in his headstrong character you find frankness of

heart.

McNaughten (genially)

I will be even with you. It's you to whom virtues are social conventions. I would praise you equally, if I had your facility with words.

Torrington

If, as I believe, we are all agreed, we can proceed.

Urania (sweetly)

No need to hurry. I am opposed, if you please, to this pretty marriage, and for a very good reason.

Hastings

You can tell us your reasons and your griefs tomorrow, sister. Don't prevent us from doing our business.

Torrington

Here, then, is the contract.

McNaughten

But, first, sir, there is a little business that must be settled first.

Torrington

Whatever you like is best. I wouldn't have been in such a hurry if you hadn't asked me to finish drawing up the contract as soon as possible.

McNaughten

Are you suggesting you've seen me before?

Torrington

At my house.

McNaughten

When?

Torrington

A little while ago.

McNaughten

Who—me? Me?

Torrington

You, yes, you. You paid me the honor of a visit in my home. But I made it worth your while, for I paid you sixty thousand pounds sterling.

McNaughten

Wait a minute. What did you say?

Torrington

You're trying to make some joke.

McNaughten

This is no laughing matter, I assure you. In fact, I am getting upset. Isn't your name Torrington?

Torrington

It certainly is.

McNaughten

And are you not a solicitor?

Torrington

I am—and an honest man to boot.

McNaughten

Oh, that's something else again. Don't you have sixty thousand pounds inheritance for me?

Torrington

I did—but no longer.

McNaughten

Why not?

Torrington

Isn't McNaughten your name?

McNaughten

Without a doubt.

Torrington

Then, I gave the sum to you, in cash and bills of exchange. And, what's more, I have your receipt for it.

McNaughten

What, sir? You have the effrontery, the insolence—

Torrington

What, sir—have you the audacity, the impudence—

McNaughten

To say that I received sixty thousand pounds for you.

Torrington

The boldness to deny it?

McNaughten

There, I confess it—an abominable man!

Torrington

There, I swear it to you—a detestable cheat.

Hastings

Hey, gentlemen, gentlemen, easy. I am ashamed for you, and I don't know which of you to believe.

Flavella

Sir, this gentleman might indeed have a heart dark enough to—

Urania

Yes, he's a rogue who glories in crime.

Jenny

Sue him, and if there's a need I will be a witness against him.

(Enter Spruce)

Spruce

Hey, what's going on here? Here's a big squabble.

McNaughten

Let this man judge of our difference. He's hardly left me all day. I call him as witness. Let him speak.

(To Spruce)

Did I receive money today from this gentleman?

Spruce

Without a doubt. Sixty thousand pounds that your uncle left you in negotiable instruments.

McNaughten (taking Spruce by the throat)

Ah, false witness, miserable imposter—you must remember—

Spruce

Yes, I remember that the sixty thousand pounds was given to a man dressed like you, of the same proud bearing, a man who intends to marry this gentleman's daughter, a man who is called McNaughten, and is from Scotland.

And, if you deny it, it's a lie, and I'll take my oath—

Torrington

See, if it's possible, to have a blacker heart, to be more

of a cheat. Alas, what are you marrying him for? I've gotten you into a pleasant business.

Hastings

I took this gentleman for a man of substance— Now, I don't value him at all.

Urania

After what he has done to me, there is no crime, no evil, that he wouldn't perpetrate.

Jenny

Traitor, finally, you're caught, and there's nothing for you to do but go hang yourself. I'll be happy to supply the rope.

McNaughten

No, I don't believe that Hell itself is capable, in its execrable rage, to make so many men, so many evil demons, as you all.

Ah, I cannot speak, I am so enraged.

(Enter the Captain)

Captain

I believe my presence is required to get to the bottom

of this astonishing mystery.

Hastings

What in the world do I see?

Torrington

What prodigy is this?

Urania

Ought I to believe my eyes?

Jenny

Madame, I don't know if my vision is troubled, or if it's some vapor, that is making me see double.

McNaughten

What object presents itself and makes me see myself, as in a mirror? Why, it's my walking portrait, or a reflection.

Captain

How dare you take my name and appearance, sir, as your own? I am Captain McNaughten, and you are injuring my reputation.

McNaughten (aside)

On my oath, this is another cheat.

(Aloud)

By what right, sir, do you steal my name? I don't go around taking yours.

Captain

I've had no other name from birth.

McNaughten

My father gave me this name.

Captain

Mine has been the same all my life.

McNaughten

In giving birth to me, my mother died.

Captain

Mine died, also—in the same manner.

McNaughten

I am from Scotland.

Captain

I, too, am from Scotland.

McNaughten

I had a certain brother, a bad scapegrace, and I haven't heard news of him in fifteen years.

Captain

I had a brother, too. A pious, churchgoing hypocrite. I've ignored his fortunes for fifteen years.

McNaughten

This brother was my identical twin, and resembled me in everything except piety.

Captain

Mine was my spitting image. Who sees him, sees me. But usually not in the same places.

McNaughten

Are you not this brother?

Captain

You've said it. There's the explanation of the mystery.

McNaughten

Is it possible? Oh, Heavens.

Captain

May this confession witness my joy and happiness. My brother, it is indeed me. What a happy encounter. Has fortune brought you to my sight?

McNaughten

Brother, there has been much to rejoice me this day. But, I rather counted on your being dead.

Jenny

All this has nothing to do with us, Madame. Be sure of it, we are going to get one or the other, no matter what happens.

Hastings

What we are witnessing is certainly unusual.

(To Flavella)

You must have one of these two for a husband. Choose the one you like, dear, and make me happy.

Flavella (recognizing the mark in the Captain's hat)

Rather than pick and choose, I'll have this gentleman, and take my chances.

(Aside)

I hope they didn't switch hats.

Urania

And me, I'll take this one. (grabbing McNaughten)

McNaughten

To listen to you, you have only to kiss and choose as you please!

Spruce

While each lady takes the one to her taste, by right of windfall, Jenny belongs to me.

Hastings (to the Captain)

Accept my daughter. Although it is pure fate that puts you in my family, I wanted a McNaughten in the family and my plans are unchanged.

Captain

In the excess of happiness my destiny has sent me, my heart is unable to contain its joy.

Spruce

Everybody is thinking about marrying— Let's do it, too—so as not to be disagreeable by being different.

Jenny

If you hadn't lied so much, I wouldn't mind.

Spruce

I did it for your own good.

Jenny

But I am afraid—

Spruce

What are you afraid of?

Jenny

Of making a crazy mistake.

Spruce

I will be making a mistake a hundred times greater than yours if I let you escape. (hugging her to him. She fends him off for a minute, then submits slyly)

(To the spectators)

Ladies and Gentlemen, as you see, I've succeeded in pulling off the marriage I prepared. I am going to bind my head in victory laurels. If I have merited your applause, you will complete my happiness. (bowing)

CURTAIN

ABOUT THE TRANSLATOR

Frank J. Morlock has written and translated many plays since retiring from the legal profession in 1992. His translations have also appeared on Project Gutenberg, the Alexandre Dumas Père web page, Literature in the Age of Napoléon, Infinite Artistries.com, and Munsey's (formerly Blackmask). In 2006 he received an award from the North American Jules Verne Society for his translations of Verne's plays. He lives and works in México.

www.ingramcontent.com/pod-product-compliance
Lightning Source LLC
LaVergne TN
LVHW041627070426
835507LV00008B/491